Conspirators'
Kitchen

presents

INDIVIDUAL TRUTH VS.
THE GLOBAL WAR ON TERROR

First performed at Lyric Hammersmith
on 11 October 2005.

Made as part of theMIX at Lyric Hammersmith
supported by Deutsche Bank.

CAST

Soldier	**Robert G Slade**
Agent	**Laila Vakil**
Waris Islam	**Munir Khairdin**
Sonny Rafiq	**Rez Kempton**
Iqbal Rohan	**Amit Shah**

PRODUCTION CREDITS

Director	**Dominic Hingorani**
Assistant Director	**Toria Banks**
Designer	**Rachana Jadhav**
Lighting Designer	**Jane Mackintosh**
Sound Design	**Simon McCorry**
Stage Manager	**Marie Costa**
Graphic Design	**Jeremy** at **Jaded Design**
Photography	**Benjamin Ealovega**
Marketing	**Helen Snell** (T.02072876889)
PR	**Emma Schad Publicity** (T.02072072874)

CONSPIRATORS' KITCHEN

Producer	**Nirjay Mahindru**
Associate Director	**Dominic Hingorani**

www.conspiratorskitchen.com

BIOGRAPHIES

Robert G Slade Soldier

Pentameters Theatre (Hampstead): Sgt. McNulty in *The Stars That Play With Laughing Sam's Dice*. Manitoba Theatre Centre: Verges in *Much Ado About Nothing*, Jim in *Humble Boy*, Renfield in *Dracula*, D.J. in *Steel Magnolias* (Warehouse). Other theatre: a founding member of Theatre X, Possible Nudity and The Smoking Dinosaurs, Robert is also a member of Adhere and Deny and Shakespeare in the Ruins, he has performed with the Winnnipeg Jewish Theatre, Prairie Theatre Exchange, Manitoba Theatre for Young People, Theatre Projects Manitoba, English Suitcase Theatre, Bear / West, The King's Players, Hamm it Up and many others.

Film / TV: keeping mostly to the stage, Robert has appeared as Cardboard Charlie on *The Fred Penner Show* and as Scotty in *For the Moment* and has appeared in nearly two hundred radio performances for the Canadian Broadcasting Corporation as well as hundreds of radio commercials.

Laila Vakil Agent

Laila Vakil trained at the Bristol Old Vic Theatre School where she was awarded the Cameron Mackintosh Scholarship.

Theatre includes *Taj* (Riverside Studios), *The Snow Queen*, *Skinny Dipping* (Nuffield Southampton), *Merchant of Venice, Our Country's Good, Pride and Prejudice* (Theatre Royal Bristol), *Midsummer Night's Dream* (Redgrave Bristol) and *Macbeth* (New Vic Studio).

Television includes *Deceased* (HTV) and *The Dream Team*.

Film includes Kenneth Brannagh's *Love's Labours Lost, Arabic Recipe,* and *Solo*.

In a previous life Laila was a Synchronised Swimming finalist at the 1992 Barcelona Olympic Games.

Munir Khairdin Waris Islam

Theatre: *Behzti* (Birmingham Rep), *Romeo & Juliet* (Hazlitt Open Air), *Bombay Dreams* (Apollo Victoria), *Rashoman* (Yellow Earth Theatre), *The Butcher's Skin* (Yellow Earth Theatre), Kafka's *The Trial* (Cherub Company), *The Merchant of Venice* (Cherub Company), *Romeo & Juliet* (Leicester Haymarket), *Sleeping Around* (Hammersmith Lyric) and *Calcutta Kosher* (Kali Theatre).

Film / TV: *Spooks* (Kudos / BBC) and *It Was An Accident* (Pathé).

Rez Kempton Sonny Rafiq

Training: Rose Bruford College Of Speech And Drama.

Theatre: *The Fortune Club* (Tricycle & Leicester Haymarket), *The Battle Of Green Lanes* (Theatre Royal Stratford East), *The Arbor* (Crucible Theatre), *Hijra* (Theatre Royal Plymouth, The Bush & West Yorkshire Playhouse), *Nativity* (Birmingham Rep), *Playboy Of The Asian World* (Leicester Haymarket), *Transmissions* (Birmingham Rep), *Arrange That Marriage* (Tour), *Don't Look At My Sister...innit!* (Watermans Arts Centre), *Routes: A Journey Of A Lifetime* (Europe and UK Tour), *Heer Ranjha* (Mac), *The Dangers Of Common Sense* (Tour), *Dear Elena Sergeevna* (BAC), *Games In The Backyard* (Grange Court Theatre), *Love Of The Nightingale* (Tour), *The Model Rai* (Paul Robeson Theatre), *The Simple Past* (The Gate), *Twelfth Night* (Millfield Theatre), *Private Lives* (Watermans Arts Centre), *A Single Step* (Tour) and *Underground Man* (Café Theatre).

Television: *Spooks* (Kudos / BBC), *Lee Evans - So What Now?* (BBC), *Trial By Jury* (BBC), *Roger Roger* (BBC), *Singapore Mutiny* (20.20 / Channel 4), *Agony* (Live), *Pardes "Abroad"* (Hr), *The Bill* (Thames), *Khula Aangan "Open Courtyard"* (Healthwise / BBC) and *Fall* (Meridian).

Film: *The Mystic Masseur* (Merchant Ivory), *My Son The Fanatic* (Zephyr / BBC), *Brothers In Trouble* (Renegade / BBC), *Recurring* (Phidias), *Balancing The Books* (Paradigm), *The Family Portrait* (Aimimage / 02), *The Divide* (Canvas), *Another Day* (Parallel Line), *If It Don't Kill Ya...* (Magic Lamp), *Spilt Milk* (Smoking Chief), *Black Nor White* (AN), *The Results* (SRK), *The King Is Dead* (Brave Men), *Loving Companions* (Exspressive), *Monk* (Imagine), *Ten To Midnight* (RD), *The Score* (AR), *Next Step* (Take 1), *Innocent Victims* (Brave Men), *The Morning Papers* (Gaz), *Scourge Of Ignorance* (Bfd), *As Long As There Is Sky And Earth* (White Lantern), *The Restaurant* (NJF), *Jami* (JHF), *Monochromatic Mismash* (Abp) and *Maggar Janne Mun* (SKF).

Radio: *The Raj Quartet* (BBC), *Driftwood Heart* (BBC), *Oxford Road* (BBC), *Paper Flowers* (BBC), *Like Another Mahabarata* (BBC) and *Routes: A Journey Of A Lifetime* (Radio Bremen).

Amit Shah Iqbal Rohan

Training: LAMDA (graduated 2003)

Theatre: Whilst at LAMDA Amit was offered the role of Salim in *Bombay Dreams* (Apollo Victoria) after which he appeared in Shakespeare's *Twelfth Night* in the West End (Albery Theatre). In 2005 he was chosen to perform in the New Voices: 24 Hour Plays at the Old Vic Theatre.

Film: also in 2005, Amit was flown out to Australia to film the feature *Like Minds* with Toni Collette and Richard Roxburgh (Gunpowder Films). Other film roles include Neran in Smita Bhide's *The Blue Tower*.

TV: Nigel in *The Afternoon Plays: Are You Jim's Wife?* (BBC); Naz in *Life Begins* (Granada).

Workshops: Lord Krishna in *Mahabharata* for which the music was composed by Nitin Sawhney (Gita Productions), Maneck Kohlah in *A Fine Balance* (Tamasha) and Salim in *Bombay Dreams: Broadway Production* (Really Useful Group).

Nirjay Mahindru Writer

Nirjay Mahindru was born in Birmingham. He studied Politics and Modern History at Manchester University and then attended Cygnet Training Theatre Drama School in Exeter. He was a professional actor for over thirteen years before moving into theatre administration. His play *Mandragora, King Of India* toured nationally in 2004. *Felling The Cedar Mountain* was a winner of a new play writing competition conducted by Critical Stage Theatre in 2002. His play *Distortion* received a developmental commission from Tamasha Theatre company. *The Bottle* represented the first play for the company he founded, Conspirators' Kitchen, performing in 2004. His radio play *The Passion Of Hungry Men* was part of the BBC's Text To Tx Scheme and he has written numerous episodes of *Silver Street* for the BBC. He was recently selected to be part of the Hydroponic programme, a scheme to promote the work of new culturally diverse writers promoted by Writernet. His play *Shah Mat* will be given a showcase reading at Soho Theatre in October 2005. He lives and works in London. Both *Mandragora* and *The Bottle* are published by Oberon Books.

Dominic Hingorani Director

Dominic Hingorani is Associate Director of Conspirators' Kitchen and directed the company's first production *The Bottle* by Nirjay Mahindru. He trained at The Royal Scottish Academy of Music and Drama and worked as an actor in theatre, including Theatre Royal Stratford East and The Royal National Theatre, radio, television and film including *Tomorrow Never Dies*. He is a freelance lecturer / director in contemporary drama theory and practice at a number of universities including Royal Holloway, London Metropolitan and Brunel. This work includes lecturing / directing on *The Missing Piece*, a joint venture between Graeae Theatre Company and London Metropolitan University. He has published a number of articles on British Asian Theatre and has contributed a chapter on the work of Tara Arts and Tamasha Theatre for *Alternatives Within The Mainstream: Black and Asian British Theatre* to be published in 2006.

Toria Banks Assistant Director

Toria first studied Medieval English at university before completing an MA in Theatre Directing at Royal Holloway. Directing credits include *Seagulls* and *The After-Dinner Joke* by Caryl Churchill, and *Stitching* by Anthony Nielson. She is also currently on a directors' training programme with the King's Head Theatre, where she recently assisted on the political comedy *Who's The Daddy?* Toria also works as a tutor and Youth Theatre leader.

Rachana Jadhav Designer

Rachana Jadhav graduated as an architect from Edinburgh College of Art and completed an MA in Scenography at St Martins College of Art and Design. In 2004 she set up Naach Theatre Company with Nadia Fall, and produced and designed *The Maids*. Her past design work includes *Slam Dunk* (Nitro Theatre Co.), *Curry Tales* and *Dancing Within Walls* (Rasa Production Co.), *The Bottle* (Conspirators' Kitchen), Under 11s Showcase (Soho Theatre) and *Trashed* (Theatre Centre). She is currently working on *Shabnam* (Naach), *Dona Flor and her two Husbands* (Dende Collective) and *In the Box installation* (Unicorn Theatre).

Jane Mackintosh Lighting Designer

Jane Mackintosh studied Art and Design at Loughborough College of Art, going on to gain a Masters in Fine Arts in the USA. She has worked in theatre since 1988 and is currently Production Manager for Greenwich and Lewisham Young People's Theatre and an associate artist with Theatre Centre, a company which specialises in new writing for young people and children.

Recent design credits include: lighting for *Missing* (Theatre Centre National Tour), set for *Breaking News* (Oxfordshire Touring Theatre Company), set for *Precious* (Theatre Centre), lighting for *The Bottle* (Conspirators' Kitchen), lighting for *Property from the 3rd Floor* (Insight Arts & Royal Opera house) and lighting for *The Soldier's Tale* (Academy of St Martin in the Fields).

Simon McCorry Composer / Sound Design

Born London 1968. Studied cello from the age of eight. Studied Philosophy at Durham University. Recent work for theatre includes *All Fall Away* (Pursued By A Bear), *Migrant Overtures* (Inhyungin / Sleeping Dogs), *Ministry of Pleasure* (Shadow of an Eye), *Mortal ladies Possessed* (Linda Marlowe), *The Bottle* (Conspirators' Kitchen), *Trojan Women* (Actors of Dionysus) and *Sprout* (Proteus Theatre).

Marie Costa Stage Manager

Marie has worked extensively as a Stage Manager and Company Stage Manager. Recent theatre credits include *Blowing Whistles* (Warehouse Theatre), *Gateway to Heaven* (Oval House Theatre & Tour), *Darwin In Malibu* (Hampstead Theatre), *The Private Room* and *Alice Virginia* (The New End Theatre), *End Of Story* (Chelsea Theatre) and two seasons with Chicken Shed Theatre Company where she stage-managed the innovative dance piece *Globaleyes* and its subsequent transfer to The Linbury Studio, Royal Opera House. Marie was resident Stage Manager and Sound Designer for several years for The Warehouse Theatre Company. Other work includes productions with Black Theatre Co op, Octagon Theatre Bolton, and Sydney Theatre Company (Australia) and productions at York Theatre Royal, Greenwich Theatre and Nuffield Theatre, Southampton.

THANKS

The company would like to thank the following for their generous support of Conspirators' Kitchen Theatre:

Thelma Holt, Stage One (formerly the Theatre Investment Fund), Hedda Beeby, Kristine Landon-Smith, Jerry Deeks and staff at Brady Arts Centre, Ravin Ganatra, Sartaj Gerewal, Liz Jadhav, Syan Kent, Nick Khan, Chris Jenkinson, Syra Haq, Ana Gillespie, Claire Hicks and all the staff at the Lyric Theatre, Diana Pao, Penny Draper-Mahindru, James Hogan and all at Oberon Books, Nick Fisher, Kate Ambler, Noleen Comiskey, Saraj Choudary, Hitesh Chauhan, Gurpreet Bhatti, Vikram Dodd, Waris Islam, Amelia Saberwal, Peter Cheeseman, Caroline Smith and InterAct Reading Service, Rob Swain, Sonali Bhattacharyya, Chloe Gilgallon, Sarah-Jane Rawlings and all the staff at Arts Council London, Isobel Hawson for her consistent support of culturally diverse work, Sian Alexander, Lawrence Evans, Mandy Short, Jennifer Kumi and Eastern Eye, Daniel Curbishley, Jana Manekshaw, Ted Craig and all the staff at the Warehouse Theatre, Croydon, Derek Nicholls.

Finally, the company would like to give a very special thanks to Lucy Taylor.

THE HOT ZONE

First published in 2005 by Oberon Books Ltd

521 Caledonian Road, London N7 9RH

Tel: 020 7607 3637 / Fax: 020 7607 3629

e-mail: oberonbooks@btconnect.com

www.oberonbooks.com

A catalogue record for this book is available from the British Library.

ISBN: 1 84002 639 1

Cover design by Jeremy Richardson

Printed in Great Britain by Antony Rowe Ltd, Chippenham

JUSTICE JACKSON: Protective custody meant that you were taking people into custody who had not committed any crimes but who, you thought, might possibly commit a crime?

HERMAN GOERING: Yes. People were arrested and taken into protective custody who had not yet committed any crime but who could be expected to do so if they remained free... the original reason for creating the concentration camps was to keep there such people whom we rightfully considered enemies of the State.

The Trial of Herman Goering,
Nuremberg, 1946

Characters

SOLDIER

AGENT

WARIS

SONNY

IQBAL

The action takes place in a prison somewhere in the world.

Prelude

Sound of a helicopter flying by.

An empty space. In its centre is a clearly defined chalked square. To the sides of the space performers sit in various positions. On the upstage wall of the space are the numbers One, Two, Three, Four, in clearly defined chalked squares. Two prisoners in orange jump suits sit by the wall. A SOLDIER approaches them and chalks around their outline. He is mid-fifties. This signifies they have to leave their surroundings and enter the chalked square, which they do. They are led to the square via chalk lines created on the floor which they must follow. Unless otherwise stated, all created chalk patterns, lines, squares or other shapes must be observed. The two prisoners are disorientated. They look around the stage. Within the square are chalked past stories of other detainees. Some in English, some in Arabic. The phrase 'In the morning we remember him' is clearly seen. A pair of empty boots are on the floor. The SOLDIER erases all the past stories, he is about to erase the phrase 'In the morning we remember him' but decides to leave it. With a stick he divides the square into two. He exits.

IQBAL: What the hell is this place?

WARIS does not reply.

Where've they taken us now?

WARIS: No matter where we are in the world…it's America.

IQBAL: America?

Sound of gun fire.

Scene One

The sound of The Chordettes' 'Mr Sandman' starts. The SOLDIER goes back to the numbers on the wall to make some administrative notes. A British Intelligence Officer, the AGENT, enters. She is Asian, late twenties / early thirties and carries a container with her belongings. She stares at the SOLDIER. In a lethargic manner he approaches her.

SOLDIER: This way ma'am.

AGENT: Is this level C or level D?

SOLDIER: Level D. Follow me please.

AGENT: How many detainees do we have here?

SOLDIER: About two hundred.

AGENT: Two hundred? In this one camp?

SOLDIER: We got two other camps here. I'll show you to your quarters. Don't expect the Ritz.

He starts to exit.

AGENT: And what about off base?

SOLDIER: Off base Ma'm?

AGENT: What do we do for recreation?

Pause. The SOLDIER looks at her, smiles and starts to walk.

SOLDIER: Follow me please.

AGENT: Is this the main holding cell?

She is referring to the clearly defined chalk square currently occupied by WARIS and IQBAL.

SOLDIER: That's correct.

AGENT: Holding how many?

SOLDIER: It varies.

AGENT: How many British detainees at present?

The SOLDIER sighs. He walks up to the numbers to see if he has marked down that information. He gives a cursory glance to his notes on the wall.

SOLDIER: British detainees, British detainees, let's see now. Yeah. Have to get back to you tomorrow on that one. Boy it's been a hell of a day huh? Hell of day it sure has.

AGENT: What are these numbers for?

SOLDIER: OK. All detainees upon arrival are categorized Level 1. This means they have the right to comfort items, a towel, a cup, a Bible, toothbrush, toilet paper, a blanket. Level 2 means some comfort items have been removed from a detainee –

AGENT: Based on?

SOLDIER: Anything. Insolence, lack of co-operation in interrogations –

AGENT: How often do interrogations occur?

SOLDIER: Level 3 represents a detainee that has had all comfort items removed but is still allowed contact with other detainees. He may have been fighting, may have wanted to start something with other inmates –

AGENT: Such as?

SOLDIER: Then we come to Level 4. Solitary confinement. No communication with anyone.

AGENT: How long are detainees in solitary?

SOLDIER: It's the real bad ass ones that go there, the ones that think it pays to be unco-operative. The jerks, the timewasters, the wanna be heroes, solitary usually sorts 'em out.

AGENT: What happens after Level 4?

SOLDIER: So you see it's a fairly simple sequential process, and the name of the game is to stick to Level 1, that way you don't need to use a cockroach to wipe your ass. Most of the detainees in this joint look like the sperm used to conceive them was one hundred per cent steroids. You do a body cavity search on these people and that ain't funny, especially when you find there's a hole in your glove, that's happened to me once or twice. Ma'm, you got any more questions I'll give you the manual first thing in the morning.

He exits and she follows. Lights come back up on WARIS and IQBAL.

IQBAL: I've shat myself... In that container...it was too hot...I started to lick the walls 'cus it had condensation, that was the sweat of dead people I was licking... I've drunk their sweat... I even drank my piss... I had to, I had to, no choice was there? Do you reckon we're on the East or the West Coast?

No reply from WARIS.

I reckon West 'cus of the heat. Yeah must be West Coast like, then again, we could be in Africa, do you reckon we're in Africa? Might have taken us to Israel, what do you reckon mate? Eh mate?

Scene Two

Enter the AGENT. She clicks her fingers to WARIS and he gets up. He then follows her to a solitary cell. WARIS sits on a chair. A light shines on him.

AGENT: Tell me about your associates in Croydon. Names, places, friends, how you spend your time.

WARIS: I've gone over this a million times before.

AGENT: Do you know Lunar House?

WARIS: In Croydon?

AGENT: Do you know Lunar House in Croydon?

WARIS: What of it?

AGENT: You know asylum seekers go there?

WARIS: Everyone knows.

AGENT: I want the names of everyone you know.

WARIS: Isn't this in my notes?

Lights fade on WARIS and the AGENT. Lights come up on IQBAL. A searchlight enters the room and focuses on him. A voice is heard through a megaphone.

VOICE: Backs to the wall!

IQBAL: British Citizen!

VOICE: Welcome to the Hot Zone!

The searchlight goes out. Lights come back up on WARIS and the AGENT.

AGENT: I know why British Asian men of your age go home. You lot always want one from back home, why is that when there's so many Asian girls in Britain?

WARIS: Asian girls in Britain have been polluted.

AGENT: Did the fact that you were adopted mean you never truly felt a sense of belonging?

WARIS: I'm not adopted.

She looks at some notes.

AGENT: We have some bad news about your mother, your adopted mother.

WARIS: What?

AGENT: She's in hospital.

WARIS: I'm co-operating with you.

AGENT: Tell us everything you know about the Croydon cell.

WARIS: I'm not adopted. Why are you saying I'm adopted?

A bright searchlight hits WARIS's face.

AGENT: You know Abu Hamza?

WARIS: I've met him.

AGENT: Where?

WARIS: Finsbury Park Mosque.

AGENT: When Hamza says, 'Wherever you are, death will catch up with you – even if you're in high elevated safe towers,' he's encouraging young British Asians isn't he?

WARIS does not reply.

He says it's his followers destiny to become shaheed and bring jihad to your own door. By shaheed he means martyrdom so that Allah will offer great rewards in the hereafter and when he says 'your own door', it's pretty clear what he means by that.

WARIS: What's wrong with my mother?

AGENT: Do you know Abu Qatada?

WARIS: Yes, I've gone through this before.

AGENT: Do you know the organisation Hizb-ut-Tahrir?

WARIS: Yes.

AGENT: Are you a member of Hizb-ut-Tahrir?

WARIS does not reply.

A lack of response is an admission of guilt Mr Islam.

WARIS does not reply.

Have you ever associated with a cleric called Omar Bakri Mohammed?

WARIS: I want to know what's wrong with my mother.

She ignores him and simply puts some music on a stereo. It is the theme of the '70s children's show Playschool. *It plays at a pleasant volume, she exits the room. Lights slowly fade to the sound of the music.*

Scene Three

The SOLDIER is at his desk. The AGENT enters.

AGENT: That Croydon boy's hiding something.

SOLDIER: Is that right?

AGENT: The clock's ticking.

SOLDIER: It's always ticking. Have those boys come from Kandahar?

AGENT: They were there for two months. Prior to that we renditioned them to Egypt, before that Jordan, before that Sherbargan Prison Afghanistan.

SOLDIER: You need to have an imaginative, let's say artistic approach to get them to talk.

AGENT: Like what?

SOLDIER: Sometimes I like them to sing.

AGENT: Sing?

SOLDIER: Sometimes. There's other ways, always other ways.

AGENT: Bin Laden's got there first.

SOLDIER: Well maybe he has maybe he ain't.

Scene Four

Isolated from the others, SONNY Rafiq is in distress. Sound of Chinese voices rises in volume. A shaft of light hits SONNY. He puts his hands to his ears, unable to bear the noise. The sound of Chinese voices reach a crescendo and SONNY starts to pull out his hair. He screams in despair.

Scene Five

IQBAL has been writing graffiti on the floor. The names Nadia and Antonia are clearly seen. WARIS is brought into the cell. WARIS ignores IQBAL and attempts to dominate the space by pacing up and down, showing no consideration to IQBAL's graffiti, and is muttering to himself.

WARIS: Should have told 'em about the computer, remember for next time, shit forgot to mention the accounts, that would have helped.

IQBAL is annoyed by WARIS walking over the graffiti but is reluctant to directly challenge him.

IQBAL: Excuse me mate, but could you…

WARIS: Don't interrupt me!

IQBAL: It's just… (*He points to the graffiti.*)

WARIS: Listen. (*Looking at the graffiti.*) Listen Nadia, don't, unless I talk to you, just don't.

IQBAL: No mate you've got it wrong, Nadia's my daughter.

WARIS: (*To himself.*) The accounts, why did I forget that? Okay think Waris, think man. We're aware of their tactics. We know what they're up to.

IQBAL: Whose we?

WARIS finds a piece of chalk. He goes to a wall and starts writing 'Waris Islam–Al Qaeda' on it. A loudspeaker is heard which shocks the boys into attention.

VOICE: We know who is telling the Truth. The Truth will set you free. Tell us the Truth and you can go home, co-operate and you can go home. The Truth will set you free.

IQBAL: How you expected to sleep with that racket every hour. Christ it's cold man! This can't be America. Where do you think we are?

VOICE: We shall be handing you comfort items shortly. We know who is telling the Truth, and the Truth will set you free.

WARIS: Halle…bloody…lujah.

Scene Six

AGENT: Of the British boys, Waris Islam's the one.

The SOLDIER looks at her and starts to giggle, which turns into a laugh.

AGENT: What's so funny?

SOLDIER: Ma'am, that's not really the point here, don't you get it?

AGENT: Why don't you enlighten me?

SOLDIER: How long you been in the field ma'am?

AGENT: What's that got to do with anything?

SOLDIER: Don't take it personally, the whole shebang. Never make it personal.

AGENT: I know what I'm doing. I *am* trained for this.

SOLDIER: I ain't disputing that.

AGENT: I've seen the horror as well you know, don't think otherwise.

SOLDIER: You seen the horror?

AGENT: Just… I want that to be clear okay?

SOLDIER: Sure ma'am.

She starts to leave. Before she exits a voice is heard on a loudspeaker. Its tone is similar to that heard on the London Underground or a British train station.

VOICE: Terrorists are reminded that smoking is not permitted on any part of this camp. Smoking is not permitted on any part of this camp.

The SOLDIER laughs. Lights fade on the SOLDIER and come back up on WARIS and IQBAL.

The AGENT enters with various comfort items.

AGENT: These are your comfort items…

IQBAL: I'm Iqbal Rohan, British Citizen! Where are we?

The AGENT starts to drop certain items on the floor.

AGENT: You have one blanket each. Toothbrush. One cup. Toilet is that bucket in the corner. One roll of toilet paper, use it sparingly…and a Bible to read.

She throws some yellow paper cards on the floor.

Here are your numbers. Chose one, wear it at all times. You'll need it for further interrogations. (*Indicating IQBAL.*) You're next.

IQBAL: Here you go.

He hands WARIS a number.

AGENT: Comfort items can be removed at any time.

She leaves.

WARIS: Hold on! Hey come back! Where are we!

Scene Seven

A shaft of light slices through the darkness and hits IQBAL who sits on the floor. Industrial sound suddenly erupts and then stops. A shaft of light hits the SOLDIER, sitting at his desk. He starts laughing.

SOLDIER: Nearly there boy! Do it again!

IQBAL attempts to perform a musical scale.

IQBAL: Doe-ray-me-fa-so-la-tee-doe.

SOLDIER: Rubbish! That's not a scale! Do it again! Get it right!

IQBAL tries the scale again.

Not bad boy! Not bad at all. You're gonna sing, you're gonna sing real good you got that boy? So let's keep this civilized and you and I will get along just fine and dandy. Once again, what's your name?

IQBAL: Iqbal Rohan.

SOLDIER: Where you from boy?

IQBAL: Wolverhampton England.

SOLDIER: Why were you in Afghanistan?

IQBAL: I'd gone to Pakistan, for a cousin's wedding like.

SOLDIER: Yet you end up in Afghanistan? You into the opium trade boy?

IQBAL: That's not why we were there…

SOLDIER: We?

IQBAL: Me.

SOLDIER: Who else went to Afghanistan with you?

IQBAL: It was a business venture… I had an idea. Thought it was a bostin' idea it was, a real gem.

He gets up and comes downstage. Sound of Asian music associated with a wedding is heard in the background. One of the other Asian actors comes onstage.

Hey Cousin! Property in Afghanistan can't be that expensive.

COUSIN: It's cheaper than water. You thinking of buying? Why not buy here, in Pakistan?

IQBAL: I'm thinking with all the redevelopment going on, I could make a profit see?

COUSIN: Afghanistan. Wrap up the wife and come on down!

IQBAL: Afghanistan. Live free or die. Okay just die!

COUSIN: Come and Golf in Afghanistan. Eighteen new holes every hour. Come on, Wedding party's gathering, might be a nice kuri for you. Sumji?

IQBAL: Listen cousin, don't tell the rest of the family, but I'm in love with someone…and it's not my girlfriend.

COUSIN: But…

IQBAL: I know, I know, fate's a bitch eh?

The COUSIN exits. IQBAL resumes his position on the floor.

SOLDIER: So you're actually a love sick property developer, well gee whiz we sure as hell made a mistake with you huh?

IQBAL: I got a good price for some land over there.

SOLDIER: Then you started crossing over the Tora Bora mountains and we know who's hiding there?

IQBAL: The Northern Alliance came along and started rounding people up, they were picking up anyone, so we decided to leg it. They took our property, they said we were terrorists. I think they were paid for getting suspects, they were just rounding up anyone for the money…

SOLDIER: Where in Wolverhampton would I get a surface-to-air missile from?

IQBAL: Pardon?

SOLDIER: Where would I get a surface-to-air missile from in Wolverhampton!

IQBAL: I swear to God this is a mistake. Honestly, I'm a nice bloke. I've given money to Comic Relief.

SOLDIER: Do you know the American Taliban John Walker Lindh?

IQBAL: Who?

SOLDIER: Stop the games man. Do you know John Walker Lindh?

IQBAL: I've never heard of him. God's truth.

The SOLDIER goes back to his desk and takes some photos. He goes over to IQBAL.

SOLDIER: The amount of aid we give you people and I have to say, never a word of thanks. Do you recognise these people?

IQBAL: It's those fanatics from Algeria, Somalia, those types of places, they're the people you should be hunting out man. (*Referring to the photos.*) I don't know any of these.

SOLDIER: Your report says you got a kid.

IQBAL: I have a daughter. I've never seen her.

SOLDIER: You seem a bit young to be a daddy.

IQBAL: See, I got my girlfriend preggars, well I had to do the honourable thing like. Then after, and this is like, just so typical yeah, I met this fantastic girl called Antonia and as soon as I saw her, it was one of those moments when you just know. My heart would skip a beat.

SOLDIER: Antonia my ass. Don't give me Antonia, you got that name out of some book.

IQBAL: It's true.

SOLDIER: Bullshit. She blonde?

IQBAL: With lovely blue eyes.

SOLDIER: You telling me a nice blonde blue-eyed girl would even…you fuck this woman?

IQBAL: No.

SOLDIER: Did you rape her? Is that why you ran away?

IQBAL: No. No sir! I love her, I would never do something like that. See I reckon we've all got kindred spirits, soul partners like, and only the lucky ones ever get to meet their right soul partner at the right time. Most of us just make do eh? I was stuck with my pregnant girlfriend. She's a real bloody bore she is. Sometimes Antonia and I would go for a few drinks in town, then after closing time we'd look for a coffee place, but that's like asking for the world in Wolverhampton, so we'd go and sit in some side street that had scaffolding all over it which we'd use as seats, chatting away, smoking fags and I didn't want the time to end. She was just perfect. She was one of those beautiful women that hadn't been out with anyone in years, suppose blokes were just afraid to ask. Really classy lady you know, her parents are doctors, she's not some riff raff.

SOLDIER: You're lying! Doctor's daughter with you? Did you sniff her panties when you raped her? You took her to this side street, with the dirty scaffolding, that's where you raped her, and she was a nice girl from a good family, raped her like a dog is that it?

IQBAL: No sir. There was a natural chemistry between us.

SOLDIER: Natural chemistry! Only natural chemistry going on there was the burn marks on her pussy when you raped her, don't tell me she was wet with you outta choice, 'cus that's a God damn lie.

IQBAL: We were friends, but I never told her how much she meant to me, I was scared of the rejection. Left handed as well, and when I was a kid the gypsies said my kindred spirit would be left handed so it was fate like. I couldn't bear not being with her so I went to Pakistan to stay with my cousin man.

SOLDIER: Ran away after you raped her. Doctor's daughter with you! Come on man! That don't go, that don't mix right. Doctor's daughter with *diplomat's* son, doctor's daughter with *lawyer's* son, that's how it goes, so you're lying jack.

IQBAL: I get a message from Antonia, while I was in Pakistan, saying she'd fallen for some bloke, I lied and told her I was really happy for her, well what else could I say eh?

SOLDIER: What guy? Normal guy? Describe this guy?

IQBAL: I don't know, some macho man twat. Never met him, wouldn't want too either.

SOLDIER: See? More lies here. He's good, he's good for her and you're just jealous. That's the truth of it as I see it. You people always wanna sniff the prom queen ain't that the truth.

IQBAL: I missed the birth of my daughter, that was bad, but the thought of Antonia with someone else, I admit I'm jealous. Love is a smoke made with the fume of sighs. Being purged, a fire sparkling in lovers eyes, being vexed, a sea nourished with lovers' tears. That's from Shakespeare that, and when we sat in the cold, on some hard scaffolding, I was Romeo and she was my Juliet. People say life's cruel, but love's crueller.

The soldier is holding a razor blade to the light.

SOLDIER: Here's some Shakespeare for you to think about. To detonate, or not to detonate, that's the question. Where in…Wolverhampton…would I be able to get…a surface-…to-air missile.

IQBAL is afraid of the razor blade's potential.

IQBAL: There's a place in Wolverhampton, it's called Molineux… That's where Wolverhampton Wanderers are, the Wolves. I'm sure you could get a surface-to-air missile from there.

SOLDIER: And these Wandering Wolves, are they Al Qaeda? That's a cell right? And their camp Molineux, tell me about it…

IQBAL: They've been looking for a potent strike force for years.

SOLDIER: Now we're getting some place. Keep talking boy.

A hissing sound is heard.

IQBAL: What's that hissing…is that gas?

SOLDIER: I ain't wearing no mask…so take it easy…

IQBAL: I just wanna go home…please.

SOLDIER: Then tell me what I need to know.

Blackout with the sound of hissing continuing.

Scene Eight

SONNY is pulling his hair out. The sound of Chinese voices are heard again. The AGENT enters. Sound of Chinese voices subsides.

AGENT: Sonny Rafiq?

SONNY: Oh Christ! Thank God! How long has it been since I've heard an English voice! I've been kept in 'ere with a whole load of Chinese people, I mean do I look Chinky or what? None of them cats speak English, one of them kept on saying 'Ficku Ficku', I couldn't work out whether he was being polite or whether that was Chinese for 'fuck you'.

AGENT: Just calm down Mr Rafiq I'm here to help you.

SONNY: Oh fucking hell what a voice! What a voice you've got!

AGENT: Mr Rafiq, please calm down. You're in safe hands now. I'm here to get you out of this hell hole.

SONNY: These yanks just move us from pillar to post.

AGENT: I know, they certainly lack tact don't they?

SONNY: This is it. Fuck knows where they send us, they never tell us. Do you know where we are?

AGENT: I think it's about time you were moved.

SONNY: Abso…fucking…lutely. Get me away from Ping and Pong, I tell you, those cats, they've put me off noodles to the end of my days.

AGENT: Moving you will represent a favour. I'd expect favours in return.

SONNY: Such as?

AGENT: Your co-operation.

SONNY: Who are you?

AGENT: The important question is Who are you? Why were you in Pakistan?

SONNY: I was visiting family. I've told them this a million times in every bloody place they've sent me to.

AGENT: Yet you end up being caught on the battlefield, within the theatre of war.

SONNY: I didn't realize I'd crossed the border.

AGENT: I'm on your side Mr Rafiq, but to be able to get you out of this hell hole you're going to have to co-operate. In many ways your life would be so much easier if you were guilty, that way you'd be out of here.

SONNY: I'm innocent, miss. I swear it.

AGENT: Look, *I* know you're innocent, *you* know you're innocent, but the Americans think differently and we've got to prove to them that you're not a terrorist.

SONNY: I'm a street warrior me, I told them Americans that, I think those cats got the wrong end of the stick. I meant street as in streetwise, hip to the groove, checking out the move, that's all.

AGENT: The Americans are not exactly all there are they?

SONNY: Putting me in with the Chop Suey Brigade!

AGENT: Do you know the American Taliban John Walker Lindh?

SONNY: Who?

AGENT: Why were you in Afghanistan Mr Rafiq?

SONNY: It was a mistake.

AGENT: You mean your activities?

SONNY: It was all a mistake.

AGENT: Follow me. You're in safe hands now.

SONNY follows the AGENT and they walk via partitions to an area occupied by WARIS and IQBAL.

AGENT: Thank you for your information Mr Rafiq.

The AGENT exits.

SONNY: Who speaks English 'ere?

IQBAL: No English here mate.

WARIS: These cells aren't big enough for three!

A voice is heard via an intercom. The tone is identical to that used by British Post Office Counters.

VOICE: Terrorist number nine please.

WARIS: Is that me? Have you got a number mate?

SONNY: Eh? Oh…Twenty-two. At last! I can actually have a conversation with someone. I was losing it man.

VOICE: Terrorist number nine please.

IQBAL: Bloody hell! It's me!

VOICE: Terrorist number nine please.

SONNY: Move it man, or they'll put you in solitary and that's a bitch here.

IQBAL walks upstage. A shaft of light shines on him as he exits.

Where are we? Mate, what country are we in?

WARIS: We reckon it's America.

SONNY: As long as it's not fucking China. She's real sexy eh?

WARIS: Who?

SONNY: The chick man. She likes me, I can tell. Women respect me. Smart women.

WARIS: Really?

SONNY: Straight up man. One, spitting image of Liz Hurley, really hot, and mate you don't get hotter than Liz Hurley, you know who she said I looked like?

WARIS: I'm not interested.

SONNY: Omar Sharif! How about that eh? Was that guy the Don or what? I mean he was suave, sophisticated, handsome, and a Muslim! See? I notice they don't put Omar Sharif films on the tele anymore, there's a generation out there that don't even know who he is! Imagine? Fucking outrageous he never got on *This is Your Life.*

WARIS: Omar Sharif!

SONNY: It's not funny being locked away with a bunch of nips you know. Fucking hell man, they've none of 'em got a sense of humour, you know, typical face of a smacked arse on 'em. Didn't realize they made 'em so tall, them cats are only half the size in the restaurants. Gave me time to think though mate, oh yes! You'll like this you will, have a cop of this eh? See, I got me thinking, when we get back home, if we get back, fucking hell, we'll have great big blanks in our CVs that'll need a bit of explaining. How you gonna deal with that bro? Eh? Have you thought about that? I have. Got myself a great idea. I'm gonna write me a letter to Elton John.

WARIS: Will you please just shut up!

SONNY: Straight up. He's a generous cat. I'm gonna tell him what happened to me, he'll help me out. Rich gay people are generous bro. Once people find out about the torture, we'll get a lot of sympathy man. You watch, me and Elton John, we'll be mates one day. You'll see my picture in the magazines. Never know, might even have my arm around Liz Hurley too.

High decibel industrial noises enter the cell. They both put their hands to their ears. This is followed by the theme tune of The Magic Roundabout *or some such children's TV tune.*

Scene Nine

SONNY is brought into a cell to be questioned by the SOLDIER and the AGENT. The SOLDIER marks out with chalk where SONNY is to place himself. SONNY complies.

SOLDIER: Now before you answer, we done question some other Brit boys, so before you open your little mouth now, don't give me some shit about you was wanting to do humanitarian work, 'cus you do that, I'm gonna put you back in with those Chinese fellas you been hanging out with. Hey boy? You know I done heard a mighty crashing in the kitchen, plates falling all over the place, ching chong! Ching chong! Ching ching chong! I done thought you and your friends had escaped! Now tell us what we need to know.

SONNY: This is all a mistake. I said that two years ago man!

SOLDIER: Sure it is boy. Why were you on the battlefield?

SONNY: 'Cus I didn't realize I was there.

SOLDIER: What the –

AGENT: What's that supposed to mean?

SONNY: I was stoned! That's the truth.

AGENT: Can't you think up a better lie than that?

SONNY: I'd gone to Pakistan on a holiday –

AGENT: Same old bullshit –

SOLDIER: Turn the God damn record over. You catch a plane from Heathrow?

SONNY: Erm, yes.

SOLDIER: What airline?

SONNY: British Airways.

SOLDIER: Lady at the check in, she was pretty right?

SONNY: Oh yeah. I reckon she quite liked me.

SOLDIER: Is that right? What was her name?

SONNY: I...I...didn't ask.

SOLDIER: Course you didn't. She wore that smart uniform though huh?

SONNY: Yeah.

SOLDIER: What colour were her panties?

SONNY: I don't know.

SOLDIER: Was she blonde?

SONNY: I think so.

SOLDIER: Course you do. So here's this nice white blonde, in one them outfits, and you must have had a peek at her panties man, what colour were they?

SONNY: I don't know.

SOLDIER: Just a little peek boy! You imagined though, that's for sure?

SONNY: She was just the check in lady.

SOLDIER: Of course she was. You're there, and you're thinking of her panties, and all I want to know is, when you thought of 'em, did you imagine 'em to be pristine and clean or did they have that whiff of filth about 'em?

SONNY: I just smiled and checked in, that's all.

AGENT: You expect us to believe you were in Pakistan for a holiday?

SONNY: It's true... I just wanted to party man, get high, see green sky, get jiggy with a woman and moan 'oooh my my' hashish man. I'd gone over there to skin up, smoke some dope without having to look over my shoulder, chill out, visit the countryside, that's the problem with London see, too polluted, I've got sensitive lungs me.

He coughs.

AGENT: I've got a good remedy for coughing. I find Ex-Lax works wonders.

SONNY: Ex-Lax?

AGENT: You take that and you'll be afraid to cough, be in no doubt.

SONNY: I've said the same thing in the other places. Just wanted to chill out man.

SOLDIER: Hey! Someone hand out the Pecan Pies, we got ourselves Honest Jim here!

SONNY: I was in Pakistan for some hash, that's the truth. I went to Lahore, then Rawalpindi, then the countryside, smoking hash, I was out of my face, it was great, the herb over there is a God send, that's why I was fucking there and that's the fucking truth. I was just smoking hash!

SOLDIER: This guy's story's so shitty it just might be true.

Scene Ten

IQBAL is alone in a cell. A shaft of light. WARIS is brought in. His face is covered with blood. With difficulty he goes and sits in a corner. IQBAL is frightened at the sight and unsure what to do.

IQBAL: Erm, hey mate? Erm, would you like some water?

No response from WARIS.

I've got a spare bit like. You can have it.

WARIS: One of them flushed a Quran down the toilet.

They sit in silence and the lights slowly fade.

Scene Eleven

The SOLDIER and the AGENT are together in an office drinking.

SOLDIER: Rendition! What a crock of shit.

AGENT: Rendition! Here's to Rendition! Three cheers to Rendition! I've never understood it.

SOLDIER: It means sending prisoners off to other countries, letting them use their techniques on 'em. That way if some guy gets his balls chewed by some Doberman in Jordan –

AGENT: I know what it means thank you, there's no evidence to suggest it works.

SOLDIER: There's no violation of international law though, let's be clear on that.

AGENT: It's in the United States Code, section 1458.

SOLDIER: Is it? Hell, maybe I should have read them rule books. Boy you sure know your stuff –

AGENT: It's all there in black and white.

SOLDIER: Although if everything was black and white, we wouldn't have colour!

AGENT: If such services are rendered by a Government agency, they shall demonstrate the technical accomplishments of the United States, such services being of an advisory, investigative, or instructional nature.

SOLDIER: That's me. I don't go in for physical torture, I'm a mental man myself.

AGENT: I'm mental too. Well it's the English way isn't it? Good old England where you can get a pizza delivered to your door faster than an ambulance!

SOLDIER: Terrorists are everywhere ma'am. Person sitting next to you on a bus, person behind you on a plane, in a theatre, that person that serves you in some shop. Man, there's more of them than flies on shit, and we're the ones that gotta wade through it. Well not tonight, no siree! Ma'am, would you care to dance?

AGENT: Pardon?

SOLDIER: A dance, ma'am.

He goes and turns a CD player on. It plays some soft jazz music.

AGENT: Just a dance mind.

They start to dance together.

SOLDIER: Of all the prisons in all the world, you had to come into mine.

The AGENT laughs, they continue to dance and the lights fade to the sound of the music.

Scene Twelve

WARIS is brought into a cell by the SOLDIER. The SOLDIER stares at him and smiles, then he laughs and carries on staring at WARIS.

SOLDIER: You seem smart enough, I just don't get *why* man?

WARIS: The West has a superiority complex that needs to be challenged.

SOLDIER: What's wrong with the democratic process to air your grievances?

WARIS: That dice is loaded and you know it. Look at Palestine, what do you have to say to that?

SOLDIER: Israel has the right to exist man.

WARIS: When you say Israel, you might as well say the United States of America. That's what made me want to fight for my brothers, Palestine, *you* know, the United Nations knows, everyone knows the injustice of that region and until it's sorted, the land will always plant seeds like me.

SOLDIER: You're not even from Palestine.

WARIS: They're my brothers. It's the one word you can say to fellow Muslims and the anger is understood. Palestine. Look, the British ended up talking to the IRA, sooner or later, whether you like it or not, you're going to have to talk to us.

SOLDIER: Well, communication's the name of the game.

WARIS: I've admitted membership, I'm co-operating. I'm low level, the bottom of the triangle; I'm not sitting next to Bin Laden plotting strategy or anything. All I do is move money, from one computer to another, ensuring cash flow for the cause is viable, I don't pull a detonator or anything, it's all via the internet, I just push a button here and there, that's all I do, well did, I've admitted it so what do I get in return?

SOLDIER: Let's be clear, there's no bargaining here. I just don't get why someone who's clearly smart, gets involved with terrorists?

WARIS: One man's terrorist is another man's freedom fighter.

SOLDIER: How big is your cell in England?

WARIS: Get me back to England and I'll show you my computer.

SOLDIER: That's not up to me.

WARIS: Well who's in charge here?

SOLDIER: Who's? Man, who's on first base?

WARIS: What?

SOLDIER: No what's on second, who's on first.

WARIS: I don't know what you're talking about.

SOLDIER: You're so young. Our friend from British Intelligence thinks you're more than just a low level operative, I don't know if that's women's intuition or what.

WARIS: She's wrong.

SOLDIER: She's a sexy lady don't you think?

WARIS: I don't know.

SOLDIER: Oh come on! Does she give you an erection?

WARIS: I'm low level that's all.

SOLDIER: I won't tell no-one. Between you and me, man to man, soldier to soldier, you get a rocket when she's up close and personal? Do you think she moans or is she one of them quiet ones?

WARIS: Just wanted to help my fellow brothers, that's our duty, that's all I did.

SOLDIER: You were just following orders, Christ that's the most original excuse I done heard.

Scene Thirteen

IQBAL and WARIS are standing in a line. The SOLDIER has some sort of baton in his hand. He starts waving it. Following is to the tune of 'Mr Sandman' or a barber-shop tune.

WARIS: Bom bom bom bom bom bom de bom bom dubey –

IQBAL: Bom bom bom bom bom –

BOTH: Bom bom bom bom oh dubey bom de bom de dom –

WARIS: Oh Mr Taliban, go make them scream –

IQBAL: Bom bom bom bom –

WARIS: You got the cutest…guns that I've seen…

BOTH: Bom bom bom bom –

WARIS: You got the training camps I wanna go ta…

BOTH: Show me how to make me those guns and mortar…

IQBAL: Oh Mr Taliban –

WARIS: Yes –

IQBAL: We're so confused –

BOTH: Bom bom bom bom –

Pause.

SOLDIER: See now you done it again! Who missed their cue?

IQBAL: I'm sorry.

SOLDIER: Can't afford to miss your cues now! Stay focused!

IQBAL: I'm sorry sir.

SOLDIER: And we need more a capella sound here.

IQBAL drops to his knees. He starts to cry. The SOLDIER and WARIS simply watch him.

Okay, okay, let's take a break here.

WARIS attempts to help him up.

WARIS: Stay strong, focus your mind.

SOLDIER: Still a man if you cry, ain't no shame in it, don't mean you're a fairy or anything. Don't mean you're a wuss.

WARIS: The real war's a mental one. Don't let them colonise your mind.

SOLDIER: No shame in being a pussy kid. Some folk are just pussies by nature, no shame in that.

IQBAL: I wanna talk.

SOLDIER: Go ahead.

IQBAL: Not here. Not with him.

Pause.

SOLDIER: Okay boy, chill out. You wanna talk, okay. Let's go.

SOLDIER and IQBAL exit. Lights fade to blackout.

Scene Fourteen

The SOLDIER is with IQBAL in a cell. The SOLDIER offers him a handkerchief.

SOLDIER: When you flew to Pakistan who sat next to you on the plane?

IQBAL: Erm, some lady, can't remember.

SOLDIER: Was she young or old?

IQBAL: She was young, I'm sure she was young.

SOLDIER: Pretty?

IQBAL: I don't, I can't remember.

SOLDIER: Was she white, black, Asian, come on!

IQBAL: White.

SOLDIER: White girl going to Pakistan? Did she wear a skirt?

IQBAL: A…yes, yes, I think she wore a skirt.

SOLDIER: Summer skirt?

IQBAL: I guess so.

SOLDIER: What colour were her panties?

IQBAL: I…I…don't know.

SOLDIER: You got yourself sitting next to this girl and she's in her summer skirt and you're telling me you didn't even take a peek at her panties? Not even a sneaky one?

IQBAL: I'm not that sort of person.

SOLDIER: You queer? 'Cus you're in the right place if you are.

IQBAL: No.

SOLDIER: Did you stay in a hotel in Lahore Pakistan?

IQBAL: A cheap one yeah.

SOLDIER: You catch a cab to this hotel?

IQBAL: Erm, yes.

SOLDIER: What colour was it?

IQBAL: The cab?

SOLDIER: What colour was the cab boy?

IQBAL: I can't remember.

SOLDIER: What was the hotel called?

IQBAL: I can't remember.

SOLDIER: Did it have a sign? You know, like a neon light?

IQBAL: Can't remember.

SOLDIER: What colour was the light? Receptionist at this hotel, man or woman?

IQBAL: Man.

SOLDIER: Did he walk with a limp?

IQBAL: I didn't notice –

SOLDIER: Give me the detail, the detail man!

IQBAL: I can't take this anymore. Just end it for me. Put a gun to my head.

SOLDIER: You people just don't value human life, not even your own.

IQBAL: I don't want to live anymore. I never really lived anyroad.

SOLDIER: Someone bring out the violin.

There is a slight pause. The SOLDIER slowly approaches IQBAL and takes out his pistol.

This place is the end of the line pal.

IQBAL: Are we in Israel? Where are we?

SOLDIER: You wanna end it right here, right now? Fine by me jack 'cus you're wasting my time. Let's get it on.

IQBAL: I get a last request don't I?

SOLDIER: Get on with it.

IQBAL: Have you a picture of my daughter on file? I'd love to see what she looks like, and maybe look at the Quran, one last time.

SOLDIER: You've intimated you're not religious.

IQBAL: I came into the world with it, I'll leave with it too.

SOLDIER: I'll happily shoot ya, but you don't get the Quran.

IQBAL: Have you got a picture of my daughter?

SOLDIER: No. Open your mouth.

IQBAL complies and the SOLDIER puts the gun in his mouth.

You never see your daughter in this life. You understand?

IQBAL nods. Pause as the SOLDIER cocks the trigger. The SOLDIER removes the gun from IQBAL's mouth.

Man, I ain't gonna give you what you want!

IQBAL: Please! I'm not sure how much more of this I can take!

Lights fade on the office.

Scene Fifteen

From blackness lights come up to reveal the dimly lit cell. WARIS, SONNY and IQBAL are asleep. The theme music to the classic TV programme The Persuaders *starts. Torchlight is seen entering the room. Two figures enter wearing hoods and holding needles in one hand, torches in the other. One leads the way as they point their torches at the boys. The first hooded figure gestures to the second that he / she should deal with SONNY first, whilst he deals with WARIS. They approach the sleeping captors, grab them, placing their hands over their prisoners' mouths and injecting them with the needles. WARIS is injected in the arm, SONNY is injected in the leg. The needles are simply pierced through their clothing. The boys wake up in shock and start screaming when they are injected which wakes up IQBAL. The first hooded figure kicks IQBAL in the face, and kicks him in the ribs just for good measure. From a pocket, the hooded figure gets another needle, ensures there isn't an air hole in the needle, grabs IQBAL by the hair and injects him in the neck. SONNY and WARIS stagger to their feet. IQBAL remains motionless on the floor. He groans, to the relief of the other two. They start to hear strange noises. The sound of goats can be heard.*

Sound of screaming is heard. The sound of screaming is intermingled with the sound of goats. The sounds subside and the sound of a heartbeat is heard. The boys start to undress out of their orange jump suits. Humiliated, they stagger around in their underpants. The sound of the heartbeat increases. One SOLDIER indicates to WARIS to lie on the floor. He complies. He then indicates to IQBAL to lie on top of WARIS. IQBAL initially resists, the SOLDIER points his gun to WARIS' head, the sound of the heartbeat increases. IQBAL complies. The other SOLDIER indicates to SONNY to lie on top of IQBAL. He complies. The first SOLDIER then places what appears to be electrodes to IQBALs' feet, and connects them to some portable machinery. The heartbeat starts to decrease but forms a backdrop sound. The first SOLDIER indicates to the second to switch the machine on. The SOLDIER complies and turns the machine on. IQBAL's body shakes with electric shock which is passed on to the others. The sound of Donald Rumsfeld is now heard whilst the first SOLDIER gets a bucket of water and pours it near WARIS, and switches the electrodes from WARIS to IQBAL.

RUMSFELD: Let me just say this, I have read this, editorials, TORTURE, and erm, one after another, Washington Post the other day, I forget when it was, just a great bold TORTURE. The implication, think of the people who read that around the world. First of all our forces read it, and the implication is that the United States Government has in one way or another ordered, authorized, permitted, tolerated, er torture. Not true. Erm, and our forces read that and they gotta wonder, do we? And as General Pink says, we don't. The President said people would be treated humanely, and that is what the orders are, that is what the requirements are...the implication that's out there is that the United States Government is engaging in torture as a matter of policy and that's not true.

The first SOLDIER indicates to the second to switch the machine on again. He/she does so. Whilst the electric current goes through the boys, their bodies shake.

Scene Sixteen

Key moments of imagery from the previous scene are repeated. Then...

SONNY: Fuck me my leg's gone into spasm man.

WARIS: What the hell was it?

SONNY: Bet it wasn't vitamins.

IQBAL: Can't feel my neck.

WARIS: It's like some anaesthetic.

SONNY: You're Al Qaeda, you're trained for this stuff yeah?

WARIS: Don't be scared guys.

IQBAL: My neck's gone 'ere!

WARIS: My hand's starting to get numb but don't be scared.

SONNY: This is it, they're gonna kill us!

WARIS: We're nothing more than guinea pigs to these people. This is your fault Iqbal! What did you tell them!

SONNY: Fucking shut up!

WARIS: I reckon you're a spy! It's the way he blinks his eyes!

SONNY: (*To WARIS.*) God you stink! That microphone up your arse is well rank.

WARIS: Or maybe it's you? Eh mate? All this time, yeah, maybe it's you.

SONNY: I was with Ying and Yong, don't forget that.

IQBAL: Calm down…it's the drug.

WARIS: Is it?

IQBAL: I bet it was that MI5 woman's idea.

SONNY: It's always the hot ones that are the real bitches, always. So hot!

WARIS staggers over to SONNY and attempts to strangle him.

WARIS: You fucking Paki cunt! What you hiding! Why don't you tell them what they want to know and stop…pissing…about!

SONNY: Mate!

WARIS: I'll fucking kill you! When you smile at her what you telling her!

SONNY: Fucking…let…go…

IQBAL staggers over and manages to disengage WARIS from SONNY. SONNY holds his neck and starts to breathe rapidly.

They're watching this man! They're laughing, she's looking at us on some monitor with that yank, he's giving it to her I reckon, I would if I was him, and he's laughing too.

IQBAL: Waris…back off…sit over there. Sonny calm down.

WARIS: That bitch said I was adopted. Said they had all the proof.

SONNY: They'll try anything. They're bound to have planted a spy.

IQBAL: Will you please just shut up like!

WARIS: Should have listened to my mum and got myself a nice Asian girl. You know what Asian relatives are like. Old Aunties used to come up to me at weddings, poking me in the ribs, you know. Poking me and cackling, telling me, 'You're next.' They stopped after I started doing the same thing to them at funerals.

SONNY: He's cracking man, fuck's sake, he's going to be a liability.

WARIS: Liability? What are you implying? Are you the plant?

SONNY: You're cracking!

A voice is heard again, the same voice as previously.

VOICE: Terrorists are reminded that smoking is not permitted on any part of this camp. Smoking is not permitted on any part of this camp.

SONNY: I reckon one of us is not all he seems, eh Iqbal?

IQBAL: Look at me mate, come on. That's it. Give me a number between one and ten.

WARIS: Eleven.

SONNY: Bloody hell he's fucked.

WARIS: I'm trained for this stuff. Trained to spot a spy too.

IQBAL: What does your training say to do man?

SONNY: Doesn't matter what we say, we'll always be terrorists to them. (*He starts shouting.*) Don't you get it you fools! It's not in our natures; you've got the wrong guys here! Well, me and Iqbal at any rate!

They start to hear strange noises. The sound of goats can be heard.

WARIS: What's that?

Scene Seventeen

Lights come up to reveal the AGENT in an office, practicing Yoga to the sound of relaxing classical music on the radio. The SOLDIER enters and switches off the radio.

SOLDIER: What drug did you use last night?

AGENT: Pardon?

SOLDIER: On the three Brit boys –

AGENT: What on earth are you talking about?

SOLDIER: Never saw you as one that would go in for electric shocks. What the hell do you think you're doing?

AGENT: I can assure you I don't know anything about it.

SOLDIER: 'Cus that's torture in my book.

AGENT: Oh I see. Some stupid yanks have fucked up on your watch, so this is what, let's blame the Brits and dig ourselves out of a hole?

SOLDIER: Somebody decided to take the law into their own hands.

AGENT: Certainly wasn't me.

SOLDIER: Man it ain't right. Those people, they're you're people…

AGENT: What do you mean my people?

SOLDIER: You come from their background right?

AGENT: Last night I was busy.

SOLDIER: Oh that I gather.

AGENT: Nothing to do with me! Where were *you* last night?

SOLDIER: Just wanna get to the bottom of it.

AGENT: Was it one too many Jack Daniels that brought it on? Was it fun?

SOLDIER: I mean injections! While they were asleep! What you inject them with?

AGENT: Must have been the local militia because it had nothing to do with me!

SOLDIER: Then we got rogue elements here.

AGENT: And you believe these allegations?

SOLDIER: You think they're lying?

AGENT: I'm saying I don't trust them.

SOLDIER: They ain't lying. Someone injected them last night and I wanna know who the fuck it was. Things are getting outta control in this zoo.

AGENT: You know what they're doing in other places.

SOLDIER: This is the God damn problem with Ghost prisoners. I've never believed rendition works, you always get this type of crap. No matter how many times you complain, you still get this shit.

AGENT: We're allowed to use whatever means necessary to extract information.

Scene Eighteen

Lights come up stage left to reveal SONNY and WARIS eating from trays of food.

SONNY: I was ashamed to be Asian when I was a kid.

WARIS: We all go through that.

SONNY: I remember when I got proud though. I was watching tele right, there was this programme on, called Record Breakers –

WARIS: Yeah I remember that. (*Sings.*) If you're the tallest –

BOTH: The smallest, if you beat them all, if your're the fattest, the thinnest, if you always win, if you're the fastest the slowest, if you really go, then you're a record breaker…

SONNY: And they had this cat on, well it used to be twins but I think one of them cats got killed –

WARIS: McWhirter.

Lights come up on MR MCWHIRTER.

SONNY: That's right, he was the cat that knew the answer to everything. Every week some kid would try to catch him out.

McWHIRTER: The tallest man in history was Robert Wadlow, who stood a mighty eight feet eleven inches.

SONNY: Then one day, there was this little Sikh boy waiting to ask a question.

Light comes up on IQBAL wearing a turban with his hand raised to ask a question.

I sat there hoping they'd ignore the little Sitarji. Thought he'd just embarrass us with some stupid question like…

IQBAL: (*In stereotypical cod Indian accent.*) Please the sir, thousand thank yous, can you be the telling me who has the biggest cock in the world.

SONNY: So he's sitting there, looking real typical, and I reckon even the TV producers thought he might make us look stupid, you know, typical BBC, so the camera focuses on the little Sitarji, close up of the greasy forehead, just to rub our noses in it, you know, McWhirter's all superior, and then it happened…

McWHIRTER: That's alright; you just take your time.

IQBAL: Well, my question is, which tree has the most leaves?

McWHIRTER: Which tree has the most leaves? Erm, okay, which tree has the most leaves, you mean what type of tree produces the most leaves, because you don't mean which specific tree in the world has the most leaves because that's just, so it's what type, is that what you're asking?

IQBAL: Yes.

McWHIRTER: Erm, what type of tree produces the most leaves? What tree would do that, let me think about this…erm, er…

SONNY: I'm sure under his breath he said –

McWHIRTER: Fucking Paki!

SONNY: He was fucked and he knew it. The cat's wriggling about all over the place, Roy Castle's shocked that for the first time ever, this cat McWhirter had been fucked. He couldn't answer the question man! The clever superior white man, stumped by a little Indian boy, by one of us man, that was the day I became proud.

The SOLDIER enters stage left. He stares at them, and they eat silently. He places some books on the floor and exits. SONNY goes to the books.

He's left us copies of the Quran.

WARIS goes over to SONNY and takes a book. SONNY takes a copy and kisses it.

Such a beautiful book man. Never appreciated it. As a kid it went in one ear and out the other, but the wisdom in these pages…

SONNY finds a piece of chalk and writes 'Sonny Rafiq-Muslim' on the wall. He then starts to copy some verses of the Quran onto the wall.

The Quran will never let you down, not like the bloody whites. This is what I turned my back on, what a mistake that was eh?

WARIS: Put a lid on it will ya?

SONNY: (*In Urdu.*) Do you speak Urdu?

WARIS: What?

SONNY: I'm not speaking English anymore. Let's speak the language of our people brother! That's resistance yeah? That's jihad.

WARIS: Please, I'm not your brother, not even your mate...

SONNY: (*In Urdu.*) See how beautiful our language sounds! Always felt ashamed of it as a kid. The English despised us for speaking it, taunting us because deep down they're afraid of us.

WARIS: Shut up!

SONNY: Why don't you speak it? Are you ashamed? Speak our language! (*In Urdu.*) It's the language of your birth, the language of your parents, so respect it!

WARIS: Guard! Guard! Help!

SONNY: (*In Urdu.*) What the fuck are you doing?

WARIS: Guard! Help! I've gotta nutter 'ere! Help! Please! Someone! There's a fruitcake in the house!

Scene Nineteen

The AGENT and the SOLDIER are together in an office.

AGENT: Lets try Sodium Pentathol –

SOLDIER: That drug doesn't guarantee jack shit. Then you get some stupid kid standing on some guy's testicles, praising his self for how easy it is to get these people to talk. Psychology's the way, it's been proven.

AGENT: There's plenty of evidence to suggest terror gets results.

SOLDIER: So you *would* accept confessions obtained via torture?

AGENT: If it takes crushing someone's balls to tell me where a bomb is, then maybe that's what we have to do.

SOLDIER: Jesus! I thought you Brits were civilized. Too many people are just plain dumb, that's a fact. People don't express that, guess they figure it don't sound right, but it's just a fact of life. Most people, on this planet, are plain ol' dumb. The real dumb ass ones are the ones into religion, 'cus they are *truly* blinded by faith.

AGENT: I don't get it. Someone like you, why?

SOLDIER: Why what?

AGENT: Why aren't you a colonel by now? Why are you here?

SOLDIER: It's a certain type that go into Intelligence. Weirdos like us.

AGENT: Weirdos like us, that's true. Guess I'd come under that category. I didn't realize it would be so lonely! Does it ever stop being lonely?

SOLDIER: Intelligence is lonely sure, but the battlefield's lonelier 'cus in combat you always wonder if that bullet's for you or the guy next to you.

AGENT: With your experience, this shit-hole, I don't understand –

SOLDIER: I made a mistake ma'am. Long time ago now. I was at the US Marine Barracks Beirut in '83 when some God damn suicide bomber blew the place to kingdom come. We lost two hundred and forty-one men that day. Warning signs had been there, God's sake they blew up the American Embassy just a few months before, took out most of our Intelligence team in one go. That same month we went into Grenada, Reagan wanted to get rid of the Marxist Government there, give Castro something to think about too. I was angry, guess we all were, I'd seen my comrades die in those barracks, so when we were there, guess some of us got trigger happy, which is fine when you're killing the enemy but don't look so hot when you kill a kid.

AGENT: You killed a child?

SOLDIER: After that Beirut bomb, the troops in Grenada were saying the most terrible things. 'Let's kill these niggers,' all that type of talk. 'Let's rape 'em before we shoot 'em,' I was never party to that. I don't blame anyone but myself, he was in my peripheral vision I just turned and shot, I don't know why I reacted like that, I was trained not to react like that. Then there was this silence, and his mama looked at me and it was like she walked in slow motion and picked up her dead child, guess he was about six or seven, she didn't even scream or yell or anything, she picked up the dead body and she held him tenderly like any mother holds her baby and she walked off with her dead child in her arms. Investigation accepted it was an accident, course they did. I see his mama in my mind every day, and even in my mind she stares at me in silence. She never uttered a word! Christ! I think some sort of fire died in me when I pulled that trigger, and a man, a real man needs some sort of fire in his belly I reckon to achieve great things in life. So Intelligence, it's like a penance for the boy, something I owe, sort of my debt to the young dead, the debt ain't repaid, not by a long shot, that's why I'm here with you, doing this shit. Man it's strange how the dice falls.

Scene Twenty

IQBAL sits cross-legged on the floor. SONNY sits cross-legged opposite him. Both are holding imaginary menus in their hands. WARIS stands apart from the other two. He approaches them in the manner of a waiter. WARIS and IQBAL adopt the manners of the posh.

WARIS: Are you ready to order sir?

IQBAL: Yes. (*To SONNY.*) Would you like cucumber sandwiches, I've heard they're simply divine here?

SONNY: Are they free?

WARIS: No sir, you'll find nothing at the Ritz is ever free.

IQBAL: Don't worry about the price Sonny. We'll have cucumber sandwiches with our tea. Earl Grey please.

WARIS: Tea, Earl Grey and cucumber sandwiches. Anything else?

IQBAL: Yes, can one ensure that the crusts are taken off?

WARIS: Certainly sir.

IQBAL: We shall have wine.

SONNY: Can I have a Kingfisher?

IQBAL: This is the Ritz Sonny! Please. Chardonnay or a nice Claret Sonny.

SONNY: Okay man, erm, let's go for the Clarinet.

WARIS: The Claret sir. May I recommend the House?

SONNY: Nar, Claret's just fine thanks.

IQBAL: I see your clientele is becoming far more culturally diverse these days.

WARIS: Unfortunately that's correct sir.

IQBAL: Nice to see the Ritz moving with the times.

WARIS: Quite.

Sound of the Islamic call to prayer is heard. SONNY adopts the prayer position. WARIS and IQBAL simply look on.

IQBAL: Bloody hell!

SONNY: Do you mind showing some respect please?

SONNY starts to pray.

IQBAL: What are you doing man? You're gonna give them the wrong impression.

SONNY: Oh so if a Muslim prays he's a terrorist?

IQBAL: I'm saying don't give 'em ammo.

SONNY: Ammo! You know, you don't half talk a load of shit.

IQBAL: Er, 'scuse me like, but stop ruining my fantasy!

SONNY: We should be standing up for ourselves. It's demeaning man! That's the point of it, to demean us. We should resist. You know what they do here, we've got to fight back. Give 'em some Jihad to think about brothers!

IQBAL: You don't want to do that Sonny, you might end up in prison.

SONNY: And that yankee doodle soldier, he comes along all smiles but my God I don't trust him.

IQBAL: He's alright. He's liberal.

SONNY: Liberal! Let me tell you, underneath every white liberal there's a fucking fascist just dying to get out, that's the truth man! Why hasn't that bitch got us out of here eh? What's her game then?

He suddenly gets up and shouts.

You've made me stronger! Hey! I know you can hear me! You won't break me with all your little games, I'm stronger now! There is no God but Allah! Allah! Allah! Allah! Allah!

WARIS: Alright man, calm down.

IQBAL: Yeah brother.

SONNY: Playing games, what a joke! We shouldn't do that type of thing, it says so in the Quran.

IQBAL: Really? Whereabouts?

SONNY: (*In a throwaway fashion.*) Erm, somewhere in the back.

IQBAL: You go ahead and fight. I just want to die. Every day I think of Antonia, every bloody day! I'm dead inside without her.

SONNY: The whites are weak underneath the mascara. (*In Urdu.*) Let's resist!

IQBAL: Stop with the lingo man!

SONNY: Stop with the lingo? Why? Can't you translate for them if it's in Urdu?

IQBAL: Shut up.

WARIS: No doubt in my mind Iqbal, you're a fucking spy. If you're so desperate to die, why don't you just top yourself?

IQBAL: What with? Give me the equipment and I'll do it.

WARIS: Maybe we can help you eh Sonny?

IQBAL starts crying again.

He's so full of waterworks he needs a bloody plumber!

The AGENT enters.

AGENT: Get ready for further interrogation. Mr Rohan?

IQBAL gets to his feet.

What happened here?

Pause.

Cat got your tongues. Did they attack you Mr Rohan?

WARIS: No-one touched him…unfortunately.

AGENT: Come with me.

IQBAL and the AGENT exit. SONNY and WARIS stare at each other.

Scene Twenty-One

Two shadows are seen. The voices of the SOLDIER and AGENT are heard. Sound of the AGENT upset.

SOLDIER: Don't get personal about this! Emotions don't come into this.

AGENT: All this time, they've known, we've had them all this time and they've fucking known!

SOLDIER: I don't think they had anything to do with it.

AGENT: Oh come on!

They come out from behind the shadows.

SOLDIER: Everyone knew it wasn't a question of if but when.

AGENT: Why do we waste our time with these people, they're not even people, why not just put a bullet through their heads!

SOLDIER: Come on, the intelligence is patchy! Don't lose your humanity.

AGENT: Humanity? Humanity? Those British boys are hiding something. They knew about London.

SOLDIER: You're reaching!

AGENT: Sonny Rafiq had a London Underground Map on his personal belongings, a *London Underground Map!*

SOLDIER: Think rationally here. Some of them have been in prison for near on three years, there's no way they could have been involved.

AGENT: We'll see about that. There's a cancer in our society and it's been lying dormant for years.

Scene Twenty-Two

SONNY and WARIS, in a cell.

WARIS: Thing is, see, erm, well, you're not gonna, see the real situation, the thing is, I work as a sales assistant for Boots the Chemist.

SONNY: Has that been like your cover? You cats always have a cover yeah?

WARIS: No you see, thing is, I'm a specialist in the photo lab, erm, at Boots the Chemist.

SONNY: Do you use the chemicals? For the bombs?

WARIS: Wish you were a bit brighter, that would really help.

SONNY: What?

WARIS: No one has ever charged us with anything! I thought if I confess, give them what they wanna hear, I'd get home see? Get a lawyer, and they'd quickly realise I was innocent.

SONNY: Shut up!

WARIS: I work as a sales assistant for Boots the Chemist, closest I've ever got to dangerous chemicals is serving the customers paracetamol.

SONNY: So all this time?

WARIS: Thought it was a way of getting out quicker, but it makes no difference what you say, so I might as well start telling the truth.

SONNY: This business of being highly trained...

WARIS: I *am* highly trained...as a photographic assistant at Boots the Chemist, High Street, Croydon. I just wanted some...respect man, thought I'd get respect if I said I was Al Qaeda.

SONNY starts to laugh.

SONNY: Mate, there's better ways of getting respect!

WARIS: See my biggest fear was getting bummed.

SONNY: These people, fuck's sake, they've got more demands than J-Lo. They'll never believe you. Once you admit to it, that's it, you're Al Qaeda now.

WARIS: People looked at me in here with, I don't know, awe or something, you know, the daddy. I've never had that before.

SONNY: You earn respect man! Earn it! Like I have.

WARIS: Who the hell respects you?

SONNY: Least I respect my faith, respect my elders, not like you.

WARIS: My mum's dead. Sure she's dead. She's old you know, she's got artificial knees. She was forty-seven when she had me. They called me a miracle. (*Pause.*) I put her in a home.

SONNY: What? You put your ma in a home, one of them old people's homes for white people?

WARIS: Told her it was temporary; she wouldn't be in there for long.

SONNY: No respect man. Boots the Chemist! Fuck me!

WARIS: Didn't think I was going to be away for long. There's only me and my mother.

SONNY: You got no other family?

WARIS: I reckon she's dead. I just hope she forgave me.

SONNY: Bloody hell. What's a hundred and fifty foot long and stinks of piss? The conga line at the old folks home.

Lights fade to blackout.

Scene Twenty-Three

Lights come up to reveal the AGENT and IQBAL.

AGENT: You're reminded everything said here is recorded.

IQBAL: I understand.

AGENT: So we should be careful what we say, don't you think Mr Rohan?

IQBAL: I understand.

AGENT: I see from your notes that you're from Wolverhampton.

IQBAL: That's right.

AGENT: Such a small world eh? I'm from Wolverhampton.

IQBAL: Don't sound it.

AGENT: Elocution lessons. My father didn't want me to sound like...well you know. Your accent is fake. It doesn't ring true to the sound of the Midlands.

IQBAL: I don't know what you're talking about.

AGENT: Drop the accent. It doesn't work.

IQBAL: This is the way I speak!

AGENT: Drop the accent, speak in your true voice, the fake accent is so unconvincing.

Slight pause. IQBAL now starts talking in RP.

IQBAL: I was scared OK?

AGENT: Why have you been speaking in a fake accent?

The SOLDIER enters and starts to observe the interrogation.

What else are you hiding?

IQBAL: I thought, well, you know, those 9/11 terrorists were all middle class, university educated, I thought, if I speak with an accent…

AGENT: We might assume that you're some thicko?

IQBAL: I just wanted to hide…

AGENT: Hiding seems to be the name of the game doesn't it?

IQBAL: I just wanted to fit in, you know. Look I was scared… Are you going to tell the others?

AGENT: Depends what you can tell us that's useful. You've been giving us the runaround Mr Rohan, and now it's time to play ball.

Sound of a child laughing. IQBAL suddenly gets up.

IQBAL: Is that my Nadia? Please! I've never seen my baby!

AGENT: Play the game and you'll see your child.

Sound of the child stops.

IQBAL: I wonder what she looks like? Bet she's dead pretty, wonder if she says 'Dada'.

AGENT: Your cover story, like your fake accent is starting to wear thin.

IQBAL: Apart from the accent it's all been the truth.

AGENT: You're going to have to get yourself a better cover story than that. We have someone here. Believe her name's Antonia?

IQBAL: What?

AGENT: That's right. There's a lot of pissed off soldiers in this camp, very pissed off Mr Rohan, we wouldn't want something to happen to her now would we? She's very pretty, you've got good taste. I'm sure the men find her pretty too.

IQBAL: Please don't hurt her. Please. Before her, I never believed in love at first sight. Please, she's got nothing to do with this.

AGENT: From the beginning, chapter and verse, why were you in Afghanistan?

Scene Twenty-Four

Lights come up to reveal WARIS and SONNY. SONNY's face is bleeding profusely.

WARIS: I'm I'm I'm I'm sss…sss scared. Aren't you scared? I've seen k…k…k…ids in 'ere, some of them c…c…c…can't be more than twelve, imagine that eh? It's the screams that get to me, do they get to you? *(Pause.)* W…w…w…w…why aren't you talking? Eh? Really turned you over this time eh? That's okay, I understand, I'm scared too you know.

SONNY starts rocking backwards and forwards.

What are you doing? Eh? Why...don't do that.

SONNY starts to slap himself on the face.

Mate! Stop doing that!

SONNY continues to rock backwards and forwards.

Why don't we do your f...f...f...fantasy? We...we...
we...we haven't done yours yet. Tell me your fantasy,
go on. Hey! Come on man, snap out of it! Please! Hey
Sonny! I'm quite shy to tell you truth, always have been,
well, when you're a kid l...l...l...li...like me...you're
n...n...n...not exactly Mr Confidence. Please talk to me
man! Fucking stammer, m...m...mama gave me stones
to cure it, stones in the mouth...this is your f...f...fault...
better not be permanent.

*The door of their cell opens. A bag is thrown in. It makes a
thud as it hits the ground.*

Rations Sonny! Have something to eat.

*WARIS goes and opens the bag. He screams and starts to
vomit. SONNY continues to rock backwards and forwards.*

Sonny, Sonny c...c...ca...can you hear me? They've
beheaded someone.

Scene Twenty-Five

*Spotlight on SONNY. He is bloody and chained to the floor.
He is singing a Guzzall in Urdu. Light slowly comes up to
reveal the AGENT sitting behind a desk. She is listening to
the Guzzall. After a while...*

AGENT: Very nice...but stop that now.

SONNY carries on singing.

Stop singing.

He ignores her and carries on singing.

I said stop it.

He suddenly stops.

SONNY: (*In Urdu.*) I am innocent of all charges. God protects me now.

AGENT: In English.

SONNY: (*In Urdu.*) I am ready to meet God now. He waits patiently for me.

AGENT: In…English…I…said.

SONNY: (*In Urdu.*) I was picked up by mistake. You must know that.

AGENT: You want to play games Mr Rafiq? Fine. I love a good game, let's play then shall we?

From her desk the AGENT takes out what appear to be three round wooden beer mats. One of the wooden mats has a two-inch metal spike attached to it. She also takes out three plastic cups.

Loved this game when I was a child. Magic, Mr Rafiq, such a fascinating subject don't you think?

SONNY: (*In Urdu.*) God protects me now, and I love you God.

The AGENT goes over to him and places the three wooden mats in front of him. She then covers them with the plastic cups.

AGENT: As you can see, underneath one of these cups is something rather nasty, and since you like to play games Mr Rafiq, then you can play this one with me.

She starts the magician's routine of moving the cups around.

Now you see me, now you don't, where could that nasty metal spike be I wonder? Put your hand over one of the cups Mr Rafiq, go on, don't be shy.

SONNY simply stares at her.

Mmm. Need to give you an incentive. How about this?

She takes her jacket off and undoes the top button of her shirt.

If you guess right, how about I undo this shirt Mr Rafiq? Would you like that? When's the last time you saw a woman's breasts Sonny. Eh?

SONNY continues to stare at her. Without looking he slams his hand down on one of the cups.

My word we are a brave boy! Well done!

She goes over to her desk and takes some plastic cups. She then comes back to SONNY and replaces the cup that his hand crushed.

Shall we play again?

Once again she moves the cups around.

Where is that nasty hard thing I wonder?

SONNY simply stares at her again.

Whoops! I forgot my part of the bargain! OK, you can look…but you can't touch.

She undoes another button of her shirt.

Some have called them ripe and juicy.

SONNY: When you look at us, are you ashamed to be Asian?

AGENT: Ahhh! So now we converse?

SONNY: That's what I reckon. You look at the likes of us, ordinary people from ordinary backgrounds and we just don't fit into your white world is that it?

AGENT: My father was a postman so spare me the working-class hero crap.

SONNY: I reckon…the likes of you would never have got into British Intelligence, never in a million years were it not for 9/11.

AGENT: My success is based on merit.

SONNY: Sure it is. I bet you don't see yourself as Asian, bet it's white hands that get to feel those fucking lovely tits of yours.

AGENT: Would you like to feel them? Hold them, squeeze them, squeeze them hard Sonny, caress them with your lips and make me groan, force me to say, 'Oh Sonny, oh Sonny, so much better than a white man, oh Sonny yes, harder Sonny! Bite me Sonny, oh yeah baby! You're so good, so much better than they are Sonny!' It's up to you but I think you're all mouth and no action. Somewhere there's that nasty, hard, cold, spike, and it's waiting for some deep…deep…penetration, it's waiting to rip through flesh and hear the moaning and the groaning of pain, moaning and groaning because it's cold…and hard…and waiting…

SONNY stares at her and slams his hand down on one of the cups. The AGENT claps.

Oh bravo! Bravo!

She undoes another button.

I believe in fairness Sonny. So near and yet so far.

SONNY puts his hand out to feel her breasts but she moves away from him. SONNY puts a hand down his jump suit and starts masturbating.

74

(*In a sexually provocative manner.*) Oh, you let it out baby! Oh yeah! Spill it out honeybear! Oh bet you could fill my mouth with it, bet you could, that's it, you let it all out. Big hot spunky, oh yeah, fucking let it out baby like you're fucking me hard.

He ejaculates.

This new found faith of yours, comes quickly doesn't it? Fancy a bacon sandwich?

She re-does the buttons of her shirt.

SONNY: (*In Urdu.*) You...are an embarrassment to Asian women, worse than a prostitute!

The AGENT puts the CD player on. It is the music of the English children's show Trumpton. *Light focuses on SONNY's profile that he's created on the wall, with his quotations from the Quran. The AGENT goes up to it with an eraser.*

AGENT: In English Mr Rafiq.

SONNY: (*In Urdu.*) Oh God you are Merciful. I love you with all my heart and ask you to forgive me! All these years I have left your house, I'm home now God!

She erases his name from the wall.

AGENT: For the last time...answer in English.

SONNY: You sanction our torture and accuse us of Terrorism? You're absolutely rotten to the core 'cus you know I've never hurt a fly. Whatever you do to me, I've got my faith.

She erases the quotes from the Quran and everything pertaining to him. SONNY starts to cry.

(*In Urdu.*) Oh God! Oh God! Protect me now!

Fade to blackout with the sound of Trumpton *now becoming louder.*

Scene Twenty-Six

The AGENT and the SOLDIER in an office.

AGENT: I have absolute proof that those boys knew the cell that attacked London.

SOLDIER: You got evidence?

AGENT: Absolute proof. The evidence has arrived.

SOLDIER: When?

AGENT: This morning. It's quite damning.

SOLDIER: Your Intelligence is on the money yeah?

AGENT: When you see it, you'll see we were right all along. The General has given me express authority –

SOLDIER: He did what?

AGENT: Express authority to deal with the British terrorists as I see fit.

SOLDIER: This camp is the jurisdiction of the United States.

AGENT: I've got no time to debate the issue, I've got confessions to get, and now I've got the proof. Look for yourself.

The AGENT goes and sits behind the desk. The SOLDIER joins her. The three lads sit on their knees on the floor. The AGENT lifts up a photo and shows it to them.

We've bent over backwards to be reasonable, bent over backwards to show you that when we make decisions they're based on rational thought and instead of appreciating that, what do we find? You boys have been giving us the run around.

SOLDIER: Evidence has arrived which casts serious doubts –

AGENT: Very serious doubts –

SOLDIER: We know you guys have been working together, we have the proof now boys.

WARIS: I've never met these guys before.

IQBAL: Nor me. Never met these two, or me, before. I mean I've met me, of course I've met me, but these two and me is a no can do.

SONNY: No can do, and that's not a martial art.

AGENT: Mr Iqbal, just drop the accent?

WARIS: What's she talking about?

AGENT: Use your real voice. This arrived this morning boys. There's Bin Laden speaking to a crowd, and look at this…look at the three men in the front row. This was taken in December 2000. We had these images analysed…what have you got to say for yourselves?

WARIS: It's not me! I swear to God! I'm not Al Qaeda! I'm a sales assistant at Boots the Chemist! You've got to believe me!

AGENT: We've got the proof, there's no point denying it!

IQBAL: It's not me either!

AGENT: Mr Rafiq, can you explain why you had a map of the London Underground on your person when you were first detained?

SONNY: So what? I always have a map.

SOLDIER: (*To the AGENT.*) Your intelligence is on the money yeah?

AGENT: Of course.

SOLDIER: Okay guys, give up the goat here and let's get it on. Cut the bullshit now, we got the proof, we got you red-handed in these photos, and our intelligence analysis proves beyond any doubt…and don't start changing your story now Mr Islam, it don't fool anyone, there's no doubt here…

AGENT: No doubt at all…

SOLDIER: No doubt what this shows, so cut the bullshit.

IQBAL: It's not me!

AGENT: We have the proof right here!

IQBAL: Honestly like…

AGENT: Oh drop the accent Mr Iqbal! (*To WARIS.*) You sir! Do you have anything to say!

WARIS: Yes!

AGENT: Anything else?

WARIS: No!

AGENT: Just as I thought.

SONNY: So what I carry an Underground Map? I've never met Bin Laden. December 2000? I was working for Curry's then man! The electrical store, so you cats got your facts wrong.

WARIS: I swear to God I was in Croydon in 2000.

SONNY: If anyone's dodgy it's this cunt. (*Referring to IQBAL.*)

IQBAL: Do you mind?

AGENT: If you just confess…that's all…confess that you went to Afghanistan for Jihad…just admit that you were low level operatives and you can go home boys.

SOLDIER: Christ, why? That's what we want to know? Why? After all we've done for you?

AGENT: Now if you sign a confession…

SONNY: I'm not signing anything…

AGENT: Which says you were a bit silly, you wanted to defend fellow Muslims, that type of thing, but it all got out of control, you never meant to join Al Qaeda, it was all an accident, if you confess, then this place will be all over for you. You can go home, your families are missing you…think of them. Just confess…everything will be alright, we'll look after you back home…away from this place…back to normality…all it needs is a signature…Mr Rohan, Antonia loves you, she realizes now she's always loved you, she's dumped her boyfriend, she's waiting for you…

IQBAL: I confess!

WARIS: Iqbal! It's a waste of time!

IQBAL: Where do I sign? I confess!

AGENT: Is that you in this photo with Bin Laden?

IQBAL: It's me in the photo with Bin Laden.

AGENT: Come on just admit it!

IQBAL: Yes I'm in the photo…I admit it.

AGENT: We've got the evidence so stop denying it. There you are with Bin Laden!

IQBAL: That's me with Bin Laden.

AGENT: Your denials will get you nowhere!

IQBAL: I admit it, it's me with Bin Laden, I'm terrorist scum.

AGENT: Stop lying! Tell the truth for once in your life.

IQBAL: I admit it! I confess!

AGENT: You're a terrorist and you've plotted to kill thousands.

IQBAL: Thousands, that's right…

AGENT: Stop lying and spit it out!

IQBAL: Yeah I admit it!

AGENT: There's no point denying it!

IQBAL: I'm not. I admit it like!

AGENT: You can't fool us you know!

IQBAL: I admit it.

AGENT: Absolute proof, that's what we have.

IQBAL: Just hand over the paper and I'll sign.

SONNY: Stop it man! Iqbal might *look* stupid, I know he *sounds* stupid, but don't let that fool you, he really *is* stupid.

IQBAL: I just wanna go home…

The AGENT gets up and goes over to SONNY.

AGENT: Why did you have a map of the Underground?

SONNY: That's not a crime.

She suddenly starts to strangle him.

AGENT: You fucking dirty smelly Paki bastard murderers! Fucking savages, I wish you were all dead you bastards, every stinking rotten last one of you! Fucking backward peasants always demanding your fucking rights!

The SOLDIER intervenes. He forcibly removes her from SONNY

SOLDIER: Okay, back off! Back off him!

SONNY starts to cough to get his breath back.

AGENT: State scrounging dirty monkeys. Stinking my fucking country out with your backward smelly illegal immigrant ways! You people are just dying to meet Allah, and you want to take the rest of us with you!

SONNY: I'm not in that photo! It's got nothing to do with me!

IQBAL: Where do I sign? Can't take it anymore!

AGENT: You're going to pay for what you've done, and we'll make sure your loved ones pay too, we'll fucking make sure of it!

Lights fade to black.

Scene Twenty-Seven

IQBAL and WARIS in a cell. The music of the '70s children's show Vision On *is heard. Concurrent with it, one hears the following voice.*

VOICE: ...stereophonic headphones...Wine Rack... Gentleman's Grooming Kit...a lamp shade...Mahogany Elephant...magazine rack.

The voice stops and the Vision On *music subsides to the background.*

IQBAL: There was no cuddly toy in that one.

WARIS: It's the same God damn weirdo bloody sounds, on the same loop, we've heard it a thousand times now!

IQBAL: Definitely no cuddly toy.

WARIS: He said cuddly toy alright. It was headphones, wine rack, cuddly toy, grooming kit...

IQBAL: Not on that one. They miss the cuddly toy out in some of them… Wonder why they do that?

WARIS: Christ, if you'd had your way you'd have signed a confession.

IQBAL: Something terrible's happened in London. See the way she went for Sonny?

WARIS: If London's been hit, well, they couldn't have been British.

IQBAL: It'll be bad for us if they were.

WARIS: British Asians can't be that thick surely? We just can't be that thick.

IQBAL: Who knows eh?

WARIS: Wonder who won the election; there must have been an election by now.

IQBAL: I bet George Bush's poodle did it again.

WARIS: You never know.

IQBAL: What I wouldn't give to be home now! Watching the footie and the cricket, that's what I miss. Wonder how Pakistan have been doing?

WARIS: Never really understood cricket. How can a game last five days? Never got that, never got the rules.

IQBAL: Stop being an idiot, you're Asian, it's in the genes.

WARIS: Don't know the rules of the game mate.

IQBAL: The rules are simple man, simple. You have two sides, one out in the field and one in. Each man that's in the side that's in goes out, and when he's out he comes in and the next man goes in until he's out. When they're all out, the side that's out comes in and the side that's been in goes out and tries to get those coming in, out.

Sometimes you get men still in and not out. When a man goes out to go in, the men who are out try to get him out, and when he is out he goes in and the next man in goes out and goes in. There are two men called umpires who stay out all the time and they decide when the men who are in are out. When both sides have been in and all the men have been out, and both sides have been out twice after all the men have been in, including those who are not out, that's the end of the game.

WARIS: Well that's cleared that up then.

Slight pause.

IQBAL: They told me they've brought someone here, Antonia.

WARIS: What was that MI5 officer talking about when she told you to drop the accent? Is it a put on? How did she know? Have you met her before?

IQBAL: I think I'd remember her if I had.

WARIS: What's her game then? I don't get it.

IQBAL: I fell for her –

WARIS: That agent?

IQBAL: Antonia! That's why I went over to Pakistan. You know, get a bit of distance like, but it don't matter where you go in the world your heart's always beating eh? When you think about it, that's quite romantic eh? Even Romeo didn't have to go through this.

WARIS: I can see the headlines right now. 'Romeo, tortured for love.'

IQBAL: She's better than me, I know that. Well travelled, she always went on foreign holidays, even as a kid. Not like me. All I ever got was Butlins and a smelly donkey.

WARIS: Shut up about her. You're living in a fantasy world.

IQBAL: They hurt her and I'll kill myself.

WARIS: Shut up about this Antonia! Just hearing her name I can tell you it would never work. Antonia!

IQBAL: I saw her sleepwalking in my dreams.

WARIS: Her destiny's with someone called Toby, or Rupert or Giles, so stop dreaming. There's something about that agent, I can't put my finger on it, she's not helping us. What if she's incompetent or something?

IQBAL: Truth is I shouldn't have got caught…you know… handed over.

WARIS: Got caught?

IQBAL: What if I was? Hypothetically like…

WARIS: Shut up…

IQBAL: Let's say I was…I don't know…trying to support the Afghans against the yanks…what of it?

WARIS: I don't know man…

IQBAL: What would you think?

WARIS: It's not what I think that matters is it?

IQBAL: Hypothetically…if I was…well a terrorist…let's use the word…what would you think?

The music of the '70s children's show Vision On *is heard again. Concurrent with it, one hears the following voice.*

VOICE: …stereophonic headphones…Wine Rack… Cuddly toy…Gentleman's Grooming Kit…a lamp shade…Mahogany Elephant…magazine rack.

WARIS: See? Cuddly toy!

IQBAL: Wasn't in the last one!

WARIS: There's always a cuddly toy, there'll always be a cuddly toy, it's always there!

Sound of metal door opening. SONNY enters. He takes out a knife.

SONNY: Look what I got me Waris! Check out the piece bro!

IQBAL: How did you get that?

WARIS: Christ sake man!

SONNY: Okay Iqbal, you wanna top yourself, now you can do it.

IQBAL: Hold on a minute.

SONNY: Or we can do it for you eh? Here Waris, you wanna do the honours.

He gives WARIS the knife.

IQBAL: Wait, just wait a minute here –

SONNY: 'Cus I reckon you're lying! You'd never top yourself man, so what have you been saying to them?

WARIS: Are you a spy Iqbal?

IQBAL: I haven't said anything about you two! Alright, I admit I made it up!

WARIS: What?

IQBAL: Antonia. She doesn't exist. Just made her up, so when they told me they've brought her here, I knew they were lying.

SONNY: Fucking weirdo has to make up his love life. Antonia! Knew it was bollocks the moment I heard it, you bullshitter. The cat's got shifty eyes man!

IQBAL: Don't you get it guys! I needed a story! Can't you see?

A shaft of light enters the stage, sound of the door opening. The SOLDIER enters. He stares at the boys who stare back.

SOLDIER: What the hell's going on here?

WARIS goes up to the SOLDIER, grabs him, suddenly produces the knife and puts it to the SOLDIER's throat.

WARIS: Get his gun!

IQBAL grabs the gun.

On your knees! Come on!

The SOLDIER complies.

IQBAL: Fucking hell guys!

WARIS: Fuck's sake get me out of here!

IQBAL: Guys!

SONNY: Allah! Allah! Allah!

WARIS: Shut up Sonny. For God's sake get me out of here now!

SOLDIER: Like I give a God damn shit!

IQBAL: Let him go man.

WARIS: (*To the SOLDIER.*) You've got a stooge! Who is it? Is it him!

IQBAL: You do this and we never get out!

SOLDIER: Go ahead, go right ahead. Kill me now. Stupid idiots! I died a long time ago.

SONNY: Maybe with his gun we could escape?

WARIS: You know we're innocent! Fuck's sake get me out of this hellhole!

SOLDIER: You were going to be released…

IQBAL: Give him a break…please!

WARIS: What do you reckon Sonny 'cus I can't take this anymore!

SONNY: I don't know! If we take him out are we martyrs?

SOLDIER: Decide whether you're smart or stupid.

WARIS: Someone's going to rape me if I stay here long enough! Get me out!

SOLDIER: You boys are meant to be released within the next few days.

WARIS: What you going to do if we let you go?

SOLDIER: Nothing.

WARIS: You swear? You're not bullshitting.

SOLDIER: Either kill me or let me go asshole!

WARIS: What do we do Sonny?

SONNY: Fuck knows man! Just don't cut his throat whatever you do!

There is a pause. WARIS moves the knife away from the SOLDIER's throat. They all back off from him. IQBAL nervously offers the SOLDIER his gun back. The SOLDIER takes it and looks at them.

SOLDIER: If it had been me…I would have cut your God damn throat. How in God's name you get this?

SONNY: We could have hurt you, we didn't. That should prove something eh? What you gonna do to us?

SOLDIER: Nothing.

SONNY: Can you help us? Are we gonna be released?

SOLDIER: Soon enough.

WARIS drops the knife and collapses to the ground holding his head in his hands.

WARIS: There's just a permanent black hole in my mind!

The boys stare at each other. The SOLDIER picks up the knife and starts to exit. He pauses and looks at them.

SOLDIER: God knows which of you's been telling the truth.

He exits. Lights fade to black.

Scene Twenty-Eight

SONNY is in solitary confinement. He lies on the floor in the foetal position. His face bloody. The AGENT comes to the door of his cell but doesn't enter.

AGENT: Sonny? Sonny? I know you can hear me. We'll keep you in solitary for as long as it takes to get the truth. We've got a bunch of Somalians on their way. Might put you in with them for a few months, how about that? This faith in Islam Sonny, is it one of your little games? It's good to have faith in something.

SONNY: (*Quietly.*) Allah…Akbar.

AGENT: I suppose people find faith in different ways eh? You know, I was posted to Rwanda straight after training. We were advising the Government on how to sustain the peace between the Tutsi and Hutus. The place was a mess, still is. I'd go into offices and watch the electricians and carpenters attempting to rebuild Kigali. The air was permanently putrid with the smell of blood. An electrician pointed out a man who was fixing a computer and he said to me, 'You see that man there?

He raped and killed my daughter.' Then he'd point to another man in the same room, one he'd been working with earlier, and he said, 'That man killed my father, and that man over there, he raped my sister, then cut off her breasts.' Everywhere you went, you'd encounter people working together, who just a few years ago had been doing the most horrific things to each other. I couldn't accept it, it was surreal, for me it just wasn't normal. There they were, working together, after all that horror. I can't be like that, maybe they're more noble than me, maybe Faith makes you stronger. Sonny? Sonny is your faith genuine, because if it is…maybe I could be of some help…Sonny?

Receiving no response from a motionless SONNY, she exits.

Scene Twenty-Nine

Shaft of light on WARIS. Shaft of light on the SOLDIER.

SOLDIER: You people think you can give us the run around?

WARIS: I was scared sir!

SOLDIER: So truth is you're just a simple sales assistant huh?

WARIS: That's right sir. Well, I was going to night school, back in Croydon, to get a better education, get some qualifications.

SOLDIER: Is that right?

WARIS: I was sir yes.

SOLDIER: And your teacher at night school, man or woman?

WARIS: Woman sir. Miss Pemberton.

SOLDIER: White, black, green, yella.

WARIS: White.

SOLDIER: She stand by a board when she teach you?

WARIS: Erm, yes.

SOLDIER: Could you smell her perfume?

WARIS: I...I don't understand.

SOLDIER: And her panties, what colour were her panties?

WARIS: I've no idea.

SOLDIER: I mean you're sitting there, she's teaching you some shit and you telling me you didn't think of her panties? You're lying, you ain't some humble Sales Assistant, we know more about you than you know about yourself and don't you forget it. That's the way it is, and that's the way it's always gonna be boy.

The AGENT enters.

AGENT: I've switched off the mikes so this isn't being recorded. When you get home, we intend to cast doubts over any story you issue, that will make your cover more believable. We want you to go back to your community, might be best to stress how unhelpful the British Government have been, I'll be your direct line manager back home. Is there any of that you don't understand?

WARIS: I understand.

SOLDIER: Don't be ridiculous.

WARIS: I'm sure I could do a good job.

AGENT: I've got Iqbal Rohan waiting to be processed. The guards will take you back to your cell.

WARIS exits.

SOLDIER: No, no, no, it's too early for him to be a double agent!

AGENT: We need double agents. My God man we need them!

SOLDIER: You know we've been duped! You know it!

AGENT: We're hated. We'll always be hated by this lot, so what do we do? Have you seen the way they look at me? It's disgusting, what I see in their eyes. So what do we do? Sit back and wait for another attack…

SOLDIER: Of course not!

AGENT: We need to go back to old fashioned intelligence. Double agents in the mosques and community centres. Satellite intelligence simply doesn't work on its own. Ex-prisoners will never be suspected by the enemy.

SOLDIER: Not like this! It's not of his own volition; he'll do anything to get out God damn it! Think rationally.

AGENT: We need them. We need agents from their community. We've injected them with Chemical 77…

SOLDIER: It was you! God damn fascist!

AGENT: We'll be able to track their movements for the rest of their natural lives. They could provide us with leads. Let them gather, let them prepare an attack; with the likes of Waris Islam in place we'll be able to thwart them.

SOLDIER: You know, people like you, they want to push it, push it to a place it shouldn't go. You're more dangerous than they are. One day someone's gonna come along and say let 'em gather, let 'em prepare, let 'em attack and kill innocent people, cus that will be the reason for the looneys out there to go, let's kill 'em all.

AGENT: Creating double agents has the backing of the General…

SOLDIER: What?

AGENT: It's for the best. Bring Mr Rohan in on your way out.

SOLDIER: How the hell you've got authorities in here, man it's unbelievable. Who you been fucking? 'Cus you must be fucking someone hard to get the authorities you got around here.

AGENT: Does that make you jealous or does it turn you on?

The SOLDIER starts to exit.

SOLDIER: You've become worse than they are, a lot worse.

He exits and IQBAL Rohan enters.

AGENT: Mr Rohan you'll be released shortly.

IQBAL: What about the others?

AGENT: Not all British detainees will be released at this time.

IQBAL: I see.

AGENT: Now your previous cover story was easy to unravel.

IQBAL: I understand.

AGENT: Cover stories need to be absolutely solid. Waris Islam thinks he's about to work for the British Government!

He laughs.

Maybe he's a double agent, maybe a triple, who knows?

IQBAL: In the game, our masks get complicated.

AGENT: Isn't that the truth? I'll be back in England shortly. Once there, I'll ensure your release. I'll be able to give you a clearance saying you're clean. We have contacts in Bradford and a sleeping cell in Leeds.

IQBAL: What about the Americans?

AGENT: The Americans are not your concern.

IQBAL: Sonny Rafiq could be a potential…

AGENT: Sonny Rafiq is dead. Such a shame. His story checked out. He was innocent all along. He'd have never joined the cause. These are dangerous times for the likes of you Iqbal, a lot's happened in the last three years, recent events in London will make life difficult for you.

IQBAL: That's inevitable.

AGENT: Drop the 'I have a daughter story', doesn't work, I didn't believe that for one second. Your unrequited love for this Antonia girl and your broken heart at not winning her is far more believable. Has a universal appeal that people understand and relate to. Don't go overboard with the 'I want to die' routine, someone might take you up on that one day. If you're going to tell lies, make sure they're good ones.

IQBAL: Fair enough.

AGENT: Our enemies think they're smart, but rest assured we're so much smarter! Insha'Allah!

IQBAL: Insha'Allah!

Lights fade to black.